Monster Sunil

Zenab Shapuri

BLUEROSE PUBLISHERS
U.K.

Copyright © Zenab Shapuri 2024

All rights reserved by author. No part of this publication may be reproduced, stored in a retrieval system or transmitted in any form or by any means, electronic, mechanical, photocopying, recording or otherwise, without the prior permission of the author. Although every precaution has been taken to verify the accuracy of the information contained herein, the publisher assumes no responsibility for any errors or omissions. No liability is assumed for damages that may result from the use of information contained within.

BlueRose Publishers takes no responsibility for any damages, losses, or liabilities that may arise from the use or misuse of the information, products, or services provided in this publication.

For permissions requests or inquiries regarding this publication, please contact:

BLUEROSE PUBLISHERS
www.BlueRoseONE.com
info@bluerosepublishers.com
+91 8882 898 898
+4407342408967

ISBN: 978-93-6261-745-3

First Edition: August 2024

Dedication

This book is dedicated to my Son Murtuza who is my inspiration on helping me getting to write books for children and given me the strength and motivation to carry on going..

Preface

This is my second book, and the book came about after my first book called Dragon Pop's Journey which is a unique and exciting book to read so I wanted to carry this theme on in all my books to come. I love children and I enjoy reading myself too and I wanted to give that excitement and joy back to all children over the world to read fun, exciting and joyful books with a twist..

Prologue

A book about young boy who meets a monster that teaches him an important lesson to see the brighter things in life - now you have to read the book to find out if the monster is a friendly one and will the boy make a furry friend..

Contents

The Boy 1
Monster Sunil 4
The Lesson 7
Activities To Do 10

The Boy

There was once a monster called Sunil who had big claws, big green eyes and hairy legs with sharp nails, and he lived in the woods in a big cave. One day he decided to go for a walk because he was bored out of his mind. He was walking for hours until he came to a castle where he could hear a little boy screaming.

"No, I don't want to go to the silly party!" shouted the boy, oh dear thought Monster Sunil that boy seems annoyed. Let me go and check and see if I can help. Monster Sunil crept up slowly towards the castle and crouched near the window where he heard the voice of the boy.

Monster Sunil saw a tall lady dressed in a long pink and gold dress with pink shoes and a golden scarf around her neck. Her hair was long and wavy, and she was very pretty. Beside her he saw the little boy he heard screaming earlier. "But mum, I don't want to go to a boring, silly party, where I will have to act all nice and prince like!" The boy said again.

Ahh thought Monster Sunil; the pretty woman is the boy's mother. "But dear Karan you have to come with me because I am not going to this party on my own and you are not staying home on your own either '' said Karan's mother. "Please mum only this once you go on your own and I promise I will behave myself. I am a big boy now; you can trust me," said Karan. "Trust you? Trust you? Oh, no I don't think so. Not after what happened the last time, young man." "But mum, you know that wasn't my fault. It was an accident caused by my friend, remember? And I am the one that called you." Karan replied.

Monster Sunil

Monster Sunil was getting tired listening to this conversation, so he started to walk away when suddenly, he heard "STOP!" Monster Sunil turned around and saw the boy running out of the castle towards him. He got scared and started to walk faster and then run as fast as his big hairy legs could take him. Karan ran faster and Monster Sunil ran even faster and then disappeared into the woods.

Karan stood still just outside the woody area where he saw Monster Sunil go in. He stood there for a while until he heard a crack of a twig. "Hello, Hello, Hellooooo..." called Karan. Karan did not get a response, so he went into the woods following the noise of the cracked twigs. Karan called again, "hello anyone there? I am not going to hurt you." Again, he heard another crack of a twig, but this time behind him. By now Karan was deep into the woods and could not see a way out and he felt a little scared.

Monster Sunil came out from behind the tall tree and in his deep voice said, "Hello Karan." Karan slowly turned around and screamed "ahhhhhhhhhh" and ran to hide behind the tree with a broken branch. "No please don't hide from me, I want to be your friend." Called Mr Sunil. Slowly Karan creeped out towards Mr Sunil... "Ermm... you... want... to... to... be... my... friend?"

"Yes, I want to be your friend because I am lonely and when I heard your voice, I thought that's a sweet voice. I think I can be that boy's friend." Replied Monster Sunil.

Karan smiled when he heard Monster Sunil's kind words and stretched out his hand to touch him. When he touched Monster Sunil, he felt a lovely warm feeling inside his heart and gave Monster Sunil a long hug.

The Lesson

Monster Sunil and Karan were good friends now and had played hide and seek, tig and tag, pirates and climbed up the tallest tree. "Now you listen to me Karan", said Monster Sunil. "You must listen to your mother and go to the party with her; she will be very happy if you go". "But the parties that mummy goes to are boring!" explained Karan with an annoyed face. "Karan, do you love your mother?" Asked Monster Sunil. Karan nodded. "Well then you must go to the party with her then."

"Karan! Karan?! Where are you Karan? We are getting late for the party." Shouted Karan's mum. Karan gave Monster Sunil a hug and ran out of the woods towards his mum. Karan's mum saw him coming and was shocked to see Karan covered in dirt. "Where have you been Karan? Look at the state of you."

Karan smiled at his mum, held her hand and without a sound walked back home with her and got changed for the party. "What's got into you Karan? I thought you didn't want to come to the boring party?" teased his mum. Karan gave mum his cheeky look and said, "Oh, well mummy I made a big furry friend who told me to make you happy, and he is my best friend." Karan's mummy smiled at him, and they both walked out, off towards their party.

Activities To Do

Word Search

T	A	B	C	P	A	R	T	Y	D	E	S
R	F	G	H	I	J	K	L	M	N	O	D
I	P	Q	R	S	U	N	I	L	S	N	O
D	T	U	V	W	X	Y	Z	A	E	B	O
C	D	E	F	G	H	I	J	K	L	M	W
N	M	O	N	S	T	E	R	O	P	Q	R
S	O	T	U	V	W	F	X	Y	B	O	Y
Z	T	A	B	D	C	E	F	G	H	I	R
J	H	K	L	M	K	N	O	P	Q	R	R
S	E	T	U	V	W	I	X	Y	Z	A	U
B	R	C	D	E	F	G	N	H	I	J	F
S	C	A	R	E	D	K	L	D	M	M	O

Find these Words!

Party	Sunil	Monster	Boy
Mother	Woods	Scared	Friend
Kind	Furry	Dirt	

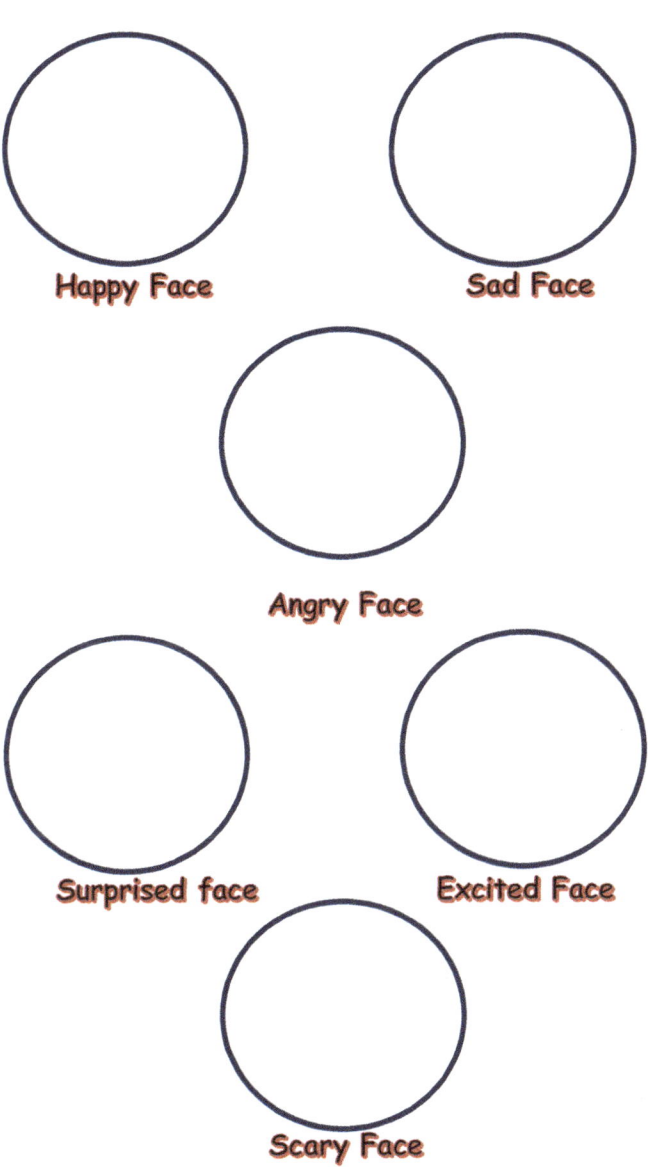

This is Sunil and his Mum:

Can you draw your family:

Create your own Monster here:

Go crazy, use paint, crayons, felt tip, pencil crayons, paper, material etc. Use anything you like to create your own Monster.

Create your own Word Search

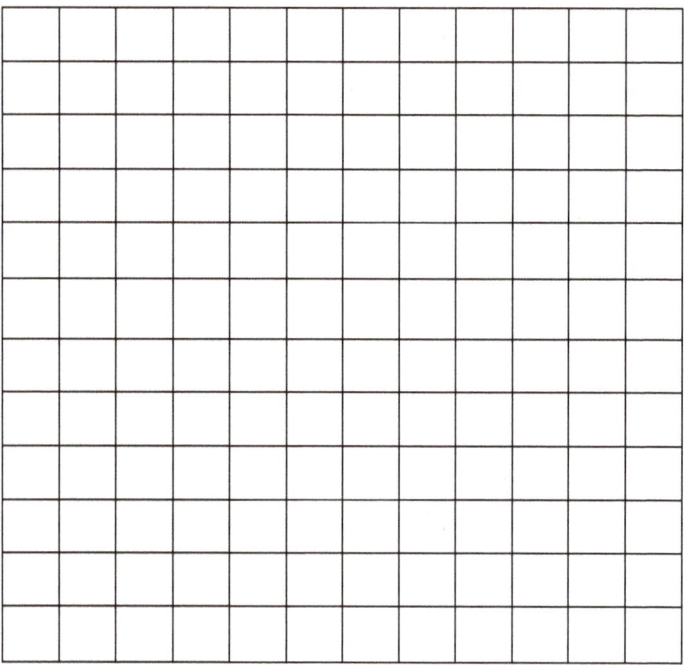

Find these Words!

Create or write your own Monster story:

What can you remember?

You can draw or write the answers:

What colour are Monster Sunil's eyes?

How big are Monster Sunil's Claws?

What colour is Karan's mum's dress?

How many teeth does Monster Smiley have?

Does Karan have golden hair, brown hair or blue hair?

How many all together?

4. If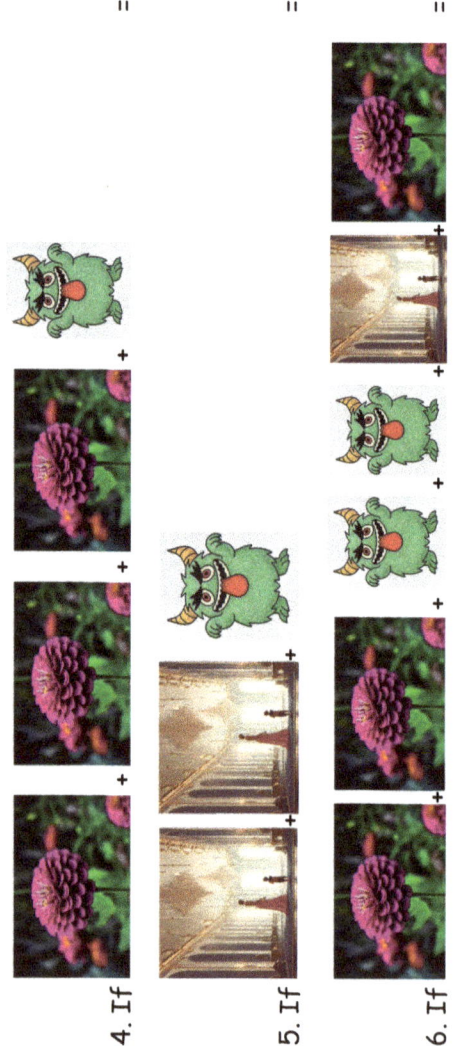

5. If

6. If

Connect the dots!

Connect dots of this Monster and Colour him in. Can you guess who it is?

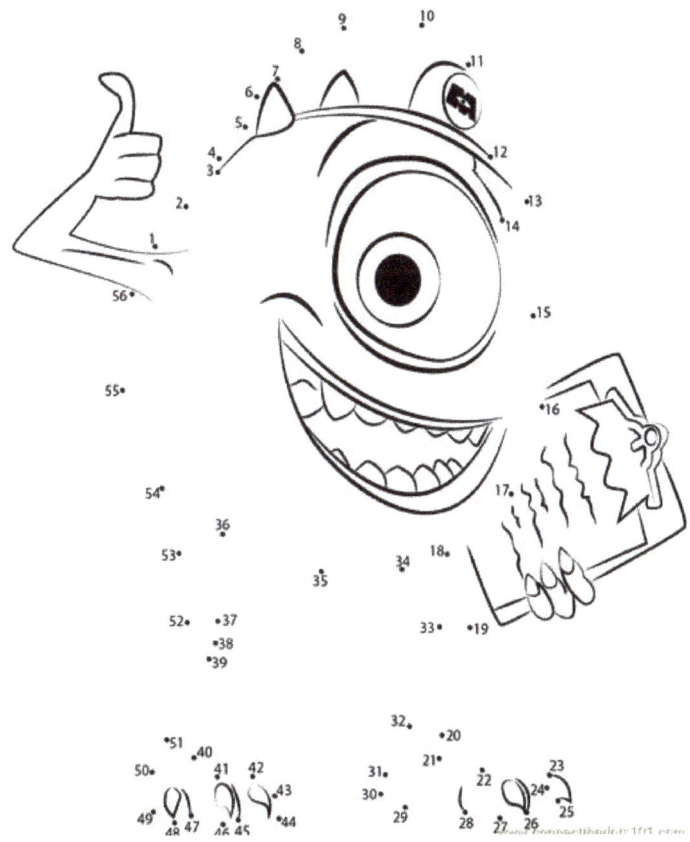

Colour Monster Sunil In

Help Karan find his way to Monster Sunil

Start

Finish

www.ingramcontent.com/pod-product-compliance
Lightning Source LLC
LaVergne TN
LVHW061627070526
838199LV00070B/6618